RHYMES OF SUCCESS

*10 Uncommon Rhymes
For Uncommon Success*

KRISS PALACE
The Diplomat

COPYRIGHT © 2022 by Kriss Palace
palacemedia338@gmail.com
All Rights Reserved

TABLE OF CONTENTS

INTRODUCTION **5**

CHAPTER ONE **7**
DEFINING YOUR PURPOSE 7
When You Discover Purpose 13
Direction by Definition of Purpose 15

CHAPTER TWO **17**
SETTING YOUR GOALS 17
Write the Vision 17
Employ Artificial Intelligence 18
The Implication 19
Work On What Works 20

CHAPTER THREE **25**
COMMUNICATION 25
Be Your Own Tout 27
Keep Your Relevance 28
Challenging Your Challenge 29

CHAPTER FOUR **31**
ASSESSING YOUR ABILITY 31
Need for Ability Assessment 33

CHAPTER FIVE **35**
PLANNING 35
Stages of Preparation 36
Necessity for Preparation 38

CHAPTER SIX **43**

TRAINING 43
  Skill Acquisition 45
  Revisit Your Course 48
  Training from Experience 49
  Courage in Training 52

CHAPTER SEVEN 55
DISCOVERY 55
  Change Needs Fresh Ideas 55
  Factors Leading to Discovery 56
  Discover People for Profit 59
  Discover Yourself for Posterity 61

CHAPTER EIGHT 65
VISION 65
  The Concept of Vision 65
  Vision and What It Takes 67
  Vision and Deadlines 69
  Stretch it Further 71
  When You Lack Vision 72
  Efficacy of Vision 73

CHAPTER NINE 75
TIME AND CHANCE 75
  The Concept of Time and Chance 75
  Recognizing Opportunities 77
  The Challenge with Opportunity 80

CHAPTER TEN 85
MAKE THE RIGHT CHOICE 85
  Choice and Responsibility 86

CONCLUSION 91

THE LAST LINE 93

REFERENCES 95

INTRODUCTION

"These are the wise sayings...written down so we'll know how...

To understand what...and where...

A manual for living, for learning what's right...

To teach the inexperienced...and give our young people a grasp on reality.

There's something here also for the seasoned men and women,

Still a thing or two for the experienced to learn (and succeed) –

Fresh wisdom to probe and penetrate,

The rhymes and reasons of wise men and women"
– Proverbs 1:1-6 (TM) Emphasis mine

Rhymes of Success is an easy-to-read success manual. It promises to add value to your knowledge for enhanced productivity, better performance in your professional calling or career, and for enhanced lifestyle.

This book is a collection of the author's ideas based on divine inspiration and lessons from his personal experiences. He also shares ideas from several successful people who have positively influenced his life.

It stresses the need for self-improvement as a necessary factor for spiritual, intellectual, emotional or psychological balance so that the individual might be complete *"wanting nothing"* in the pursuit of their future prospects and the purposes of God.

Rhymes of Success is a must-read for everyone who yearns for fresh insights, undiluted information, and a new level in life. It is incisive, inspiring, and intact such that you will find fulfilment going through it. Happy reading and **SUCCEED**!

Kriss Palace

CHAPTER ONE

DEFINING YOUR PURPOSE

*"**There are many devices in a man's heart; nevertheless the counsel of the LORD, that shall stand**"* Proverbs 19:21

Myles Munroe once said, **"If purpose is not known, abuse is inevitable"**. God created every human being with a purpose. He has a plan for you. There is no one God created without a blueprint. Even a child born out of wedlock or the one born by a careless girl who cannot even remember the man responsible for her pregnancy – people call such a bastard child – all have their purpose in life. So long they are human beings in the "image" of God, there is a plan for them.

However each person's purpose as designed by their Creator is uniquely different from the others. Hence, every man must know and understand what that divine plan or purpose is, and should strive to know its details in order to fulfil it.

Before you can begin to plan to achieve anything in life, you need to discover what God designed you to be and to do. After this, you can then plan your life based on that discovery.

Now, the question: What do you plan to achieve in life? Is it in affinity with the purpose of God? Have you discovered it or yet to do so? It takes a sincere heart to discover destiny and God's purpose. When this is done, it will lead you to develop focus.

To define your purpose means that you begin to understand the what (task), where (place), how (means/methods), with whom (partners), and the why (reasons) of your life on earth. Let me explain further.

1. You have a task to accomplish. Every form of invention whether machine or material has a task to accomplish. No machine was designed for nothing. So also every human being has a task, a job description, something of worth to start and finish. You must come to a point where you are convinced of that discovery and really know it.

2. There is a place to accomplish it. When God created and made the first humans, He put them in a Garden called Eden. He did not put them on the moon to start reading the stars or gazing at the moon or empty space around it. God gave them a job description which they should do within the environment where God put them.

   You too have a place to carry out your divine assignment. Everywhere is nowhere! There is a place of execution of the task in order for accomplishment to become a reality. So many people are not where they are purposed by God to be so they labor without commensurate fruit because they are working other people's farm lands. You must seek to discover your place of assignment and relevance in life.

3. There are methods of accomplishing the purpose. Not all options are open to you. Whatever means God has given you must favor the task. In Exodus 25:9; 26:30, when God commanded Moses to build the tabernacle in the wilderness, He gave him the model and the modus operandi. When

God gave commandments for the offering of sacrifices, He gave the modus operandi.

Every job description has a model and modus operandi for getting it done. Resources will only be released to you to accomplish your task when you know how to use them efficiently well. Otherwise, you end up misusing them and achieving nothing. Most of our problems arise from not knowing how to use available resources to achieve best results.

4. There is a reason for the task to be accomplished not just by anybody but by YOU. Each man is specially designed for something unique. Just as the eye cannot carry out the function of the nose and vice versa, you are not created for anyhow task. Whether at a higher dimension or not, you are just custom-made for that assignment. So, do not despise your assignment no matter how odd or menial it might appear. Instead show some gratitude. The fact remains God chose you to do it, and that is what counts.

5. There are people that have been ordained to partner or help you accomplish the task. Back to Moses again. God specifically anointed Bezalel and Oholiab with excellent spirit of craftsmanship to help him build the tabernacle. Most people fail to accomplish much of their assignment in life because they either choose the wrong people or reject the right people God brings to them.

   Adam was made first. But for partnership and procreation, God made Eve and introduced her to Adam. Adam would have failed to produce offspring that are completely human if he married any of the apes just because they looked alike. You too will fail if you do not hook up with the right people in executing your divine mandate. Some purposes have been defeated because of wrong partnerships.

6. There are people who must benefit from the execution of those tasks. We do not live for ourselves. Everyone here on planet earth is either a product manufacturer or a service provider. Whatever you do, bear in mind that there are

beneficiaries and consumers. This is one of the cardinals of your purpose.

You must discover who the consumers and beneficiaries of your products or services are so you channel your resources in the right direction. By doing this, you receive adequate response from them. We often receive cold shoulders because we lean on the wrong people. We also receive poor patronage when we advertise to the wrong customers.

Note that not everyone will understand you from the beginning. And when people around you especially those with whom you must accomplish the purpose do not seem to understand the assignment, then grab the initiative and explain it to them. This is the point where defining your purpose becomes very demanding on you. The essence of doing so cannot be overemphasized as it holds the key to your fulfilment in life. You must take responsibility of getting it right from the start otherwise you might get stuck when defining or trying moments come.

Take note also that you cannot achieve greatness if you do not get it right from the beginning and this means getting some things straightened out. This is because responsibility is a major price we pay to achieve greatness. Do not shift it to others no matter how much they are willing to contribute to your destiny. They are only your destiny-helpers and not your destiny holders! They are passengers not the pilots of your life!

Remember that God called you, and they were not there when He did. So they do not really know the details of God's purpose and plans for your life, you alone do. If you allow them, they might take the wrong lead and the wrong turns, and things will definitely go wrong. Therefore take the lead and the responsibility of letting them in when necessary. If they are the right people to partner with or benefit from you, they will stay. But do not let them take over. Be in charge!

When You Discover Purpose

A man cannot succeed without first discovering and defining his purpose - the blueprint of his God-given life. This is because many things happen when purpose is discovered. These are as follow:

- ❖ It awakens the giant in you. The drive for accomplishment will not be awakened until you discover what is designed to drive you.
- ❖ It lets you have a conviction of what you will be. A discovery of purpose is a discovery of personality. Your real self will remain hidden until you find what you are born to do and be.
- ❖ Knowing the blueprint of your life helps you discover your unique style and ingenuity. You will remain a formatted copy of someone else until you discover what your true identity.
- ❖ It also makes your packaging easy. Emulation is good, imitation is abuse of who you are and it brings limitation. So watch it.
- ❖ Finally, it makes you receive fire and passion to achieve your vision.

In Luke 4:16-22, a story was told about Jesus Christ. Searching the scriptures, He found a place it was written of Him; His purpose. There, Jesus read it out;

making it known to all. His goal in life was explicitly defined.

Direction by Definition of Purpose

When you properly understand your purpose in life, getting direction becomes easy. Since God is the Designer of the blueprint of your life, he alone provides guidance to fulfilling it. But He can only give attention to the man or woman who is focused. That is, the man or woman who sticks to His plan even against all odds will get attention.

Truth is that trying moments will show up in the life of such a man to test where he stands. Some people are going to be used to try to confuse you to choose a different path from what your Creator plans for you. You must do all in your power with the grace of God that is readily available to resist it.

During this time, some people around may begin to question your credibility in comparison to your personality or background. They may do this by their actions toward you or by speaking it out. Do not be swayed by that; it is inevitable in life. In fact, if no one questions your credibility or believability, it means they are still studying you or you are not pursuing the right destiny. Every day, people question God's rule over the universe. Moses was questioned too. The prophets were also challenged and so they did to Jesus Christ.

Talking about Jesus, the Holy Bible said that immediately He finished reading the scriptures, all eyes were fixed on Him. Then the question: **"Is this not the son of Joseph...?"** They tried to size Him up; to figure out how possible that the son of a carpenter could have such unparalleled knowledge. If they did so to the Master, remember, they will do so to you. But He held on to the plan of God. So, do must do the same.

So, keeping tabs with the reason for God's purpose for your life will help you stay on course. If you have found out His plans for your life, focus on it and pursue it until you accomplish it. Nothing more is worth living for than this!

CHAPTER TWO

SETTING YOUR GOALS

"But this one thing I do, forgetting the things which are behind and focusing on things which are ahead" Philippians 3:13

Now that you have known your purpose and have been able to get it well defined, let us look at how you can go about achieving it. This starts with setting goals. You must have a plan to accomplish the plan of God. The understanding of this is very vital to accomplishing the very purpose or plan or intention God has in creating you.

Write the Vision

To set a goal means to break down the plan in bits and sequence. There must be what to do first and what to do follow. The first should not come last and the last thing should not come at the beginning. Some people get confused when it comes to arranging these goals in a good order. You should not get confused if you already know what to do and how to do it. What this means is that you must strive to get the whole picture and put it down on paper. **"Write the vision and make it plain on paper..."** (Habakkuk 2:2).

You have to first of all understand that the setting your goals is not an end but a means to an end. It is to help and guide you in knowing how far you can go and how well you are doing in achieving your plans. Whatever your goals are, and whatever you do, make sure they stem from that singular purpose and central will of God. "**The purposes of a man's heart are deep waters, but one who has insight draws them out**" Proverbs 20:5 NIV.

Employ Artificial Intelligence

The proverb above says a lot about this. You must set goals that come from your understanding of the purpose, of course. If your understanding is shallow, the danger is that you will set wrong, unattainable goals. But if it is intact, then the work becomes easy for you. One important factor is needed here, and that is *insight*. In artificial intelligence, this means an extended comprehension of a subject matter which results from identifying the relationships and behaviors within a context. You must see the interior, see intuitively and deduct the core essential of why you are here on earth. For Apostle Paul, nothing else mattered but that **"one thing"**.

This is not only for your benefit but for others too. You must clarify your objectives or goals especially for those partners or destiny helpers. This will help you communicate effectively with them in achieving its fulfilment.

The Implication

Setting your goals will help you in taking care of other issues outside the core objective that might crop up in the process of time. These other issues if allowed might swallow, scuttle or circumvent the original divine agenda for your life. It is expected that the divine plan or the understanding of it should come as a revelation from God your Creator but it may take a higher level of spiritual intimacy with Him and great commitment to comprehend its components.

This is very important as it takes a deeper revelation to understand and adequately expound a revelation. It also takes a good understanding of the revealed plan to create and establish factors that will bring about its accomplishment. With these known and established, you must aim at something; something concrete and realistic. You do not need to hurry it because in the process, you will learn to work on what really works!

Work On What Works

Your goals must be set on what you deduce from insight that will work. Not everything will work. This is crucial because as you get to understand your core assignment, you learn to pin it down to what really works else you are in danger of muddling together both the workable and the not workable aspects. This is to say you structure and streamline them where necessary.

Listen: You will have no real destination if you do not have a given direction. There is always a map. Apostle Paul said, **"But one thing I do: ...I press on toward the goal..."** (Philippians 3:13-14 NIV) The Message

Bible renders it this way: ***"But I've got my eye on the goal."*** Following his example will lessen the distractions on the way.

Now, that is it! You must get your eye on one thing. For example, if you are called to be a medical doctor, you must know which part of the medical profession you are called and equipped to function in. Your goal must be to throw yourself right into that part and not to juggle from pediatrics, for instance, to gynecology, dentistry, or surgery.

If you are ordained to be a manufacturer of products, you must get to know which products to focus on and what purpose they serve. Some people manufacturer automobile and their parts while some produce household things. You may not be designed and equipped to be a manufacturer of everything. Even though it is not a crime to do this but finding what you are equipped for will make it easier when setting goals to achieve them.

You may ask, how do I get to know all these things? Simple: Ask the One who designed you. Follow your heart, too. And think deeply of the things that bring maximum satisfaction and fulfilment to you. That thing that pops up joy and excitement in your heart is more likely to be your calling in life. Go for it!

As a service provider, I love seeing people prosper in life. I have many skills but I realize with the passage of time that I get super excited when I see people who have poor knowledge of things climb the stairs of knowledge. So I find that I need to help them raise their knowledge bar so they can rise in life. This helps me to do more in providing them with information that increases their knowledge to succeed in their own fields.

If you are called as a priest or pastor, find out what one thing you should do in the ministry. This is not to say that you have only one part of the purpose, but that you find the primary before engaging in the supportive or secondary.

When get it in this way, it automatically helps you. It means that you now have something to look forward to accomplish within a time frame. That is, you create deadlines. You become more focused, and save energy to pursue and accomplish greater things.

Working on what works is akin to setting goals that are realistic within the confines of your purpose. The following happen:

⇒ You create more room for external involvement and investment.

⇒ You become largely free from unnecessary entanglements and estrangement.

⇒ You command more attention and attraction, and you grow.

So setting of goals is very important so you can do the right thing and win always.

CHAPTER THREE

COMMUNICATION

'Hello!' I guess you replied, 'Hello'. That is communication. I call, you respond. What you have in mind, you let out of your mouth. Let someone know about it. Show it. Placard it. Shut mouth is shut destiny. But before you do that, be cautious. There are rules of engagement. You should know them before you engage.

First take a good long look at yourself. Who are you? What is your personality? What is your brand? Do you look like what or who you claim to be? Are you a professional or do you just think so? There is a difference between thinking so and knowing so. For example, I am the 'The diplomat'. I do not claim to be because I think so, but because I know that I am. You must know the difference before you say it.

You can communicate through your image, personality or brand. These must cover the following aspects of your business:

⇒ Personal image

⇒ Packaging or branding of your product or service

⇒ Provision of information for the customer or clientele.

If any of the above mentioned areas is below average, it will affect your communication lifestyle. What this translates to is if your dressing is bad, you are not punctual, and you miss appointments, you are simply sending out the wrong messages.

If you do not keep up at meetings, or your office your office has a poor and lousy correspondence, you will terribly suffer the consequence. So if all these areas are in the negative, you equally attract negative feedback. You must take this seriously. Even if you are not a trained professional, you should attempt to look professional by careful observation. Look at those ahead of you in this regard, copy and then modify to suit your personality.

Be Your Own Tout

You will not go far in life if you do not learn to speak out or advertise yourself. God told Prophet Habakkuk to write the vision and make it plain so anyone could read it on the move. We often suffer low patronage because we do not adequately advertise our products and services. Even in the family, when the father does not effectively communicate his vision to his family members, say his wife and children, they tend to be indifferent to his pursuits. Successful people are known for effective communication of their programs to those they believe would patronize them. Successful corporations equally do a lot of advertising to get and enjoy great patronage. They do not stop advertising their brands even when they have become popular brands.

Politicians use people on the streets to draw crowd to themselves and sell their manifesto. You cannot go far in the pursuit of your purpose without outreach. If you must reach out, then you must as a necessity embark on targeted outreach. According to one of my favorite motivational speakers and career-success coaches in Africa, Muyiwa Afolabi, you need to be your own tout to succeed in business and career.

In fact, I did not learn this early in life because we were taught not to blow our trumpet. So later in life when I began to 'blow my trumpet' and people would tell me to slow down, I tell them that I slowed down for years and never achieved much. When you are enjoying a movie, you would not want anyone to pause it unnecessarily or take you back. You want to enjoy the flow to the end.

Keep Your Relevance

You do not quit after a win. You want to keep winning, right? So even if your product or service has been well received in the market place, the need to keep pushing it is key to remaining in the mainstream. We only knew the God of Abraham, Isaac and Jacob. Not as I AM. But when He met with Moses centuries later, He introduced Himself as I AM that I AM. That is keeping His relevance.

He never let Moses discover Him and He still does the same today. He came looking for us. We never took the initiative to look for Him, we only respond. Looking for God is religion while God comes seeking to reconcile man to Himself is Christianity. So, do not wait until people ask you what business you are doing; grab the initiative to inform them and urge them to patronize you. That is key to becoming successful in life.

Challenging Your Challenge

It can be so hard for some people to do this. When you have been taught to maintain status quo, it is a challenge to adjust to the new. And when you decide to give it a try, you always come up with the question: 'But how can I?' Tony Robbins said, **"It is not a question of can you, but will you?"**

This is how it works. **"Do the thing and you will have the power"**, Ralph Waldo Emerson. There is a surge of confidence that flows in you once you make the first move and succeed no matter how little. Then, you will doubtless receive the power to do more!

Take this advice: You must not discuss your business or career goals with carelessness and pessimism, rather you must talk faith. It is not because you want to brag, show off or deceive people into believing in you but because you strongly believe that you have what it takes to deliver expectations. Of course, you will succeed! After all, if you can consistently dream about it, think about it, and pursue it, you will surely achieve it.

CHAPTER FOUR

ASSESSING YOUR ABILITY

There is ability in you that is seeking expression. When you get the right platform, you show what you have got inside you. Most of the times, it is the ability that is expressed that attracts the platform. So until you begin to express yourself from where you are, you may not get to where you want to be next. Truth is, a platform is already waiting for you.

There is a measure of faith and grace given to you to accomplish the given task and succeed in life. You may not be able to add to that measure but you should maintain and nurture the faith and grace. A lot of people think that engaging in unrealistic tasks is a demonstration of faith. Not quite. God knows your ability but it will be nice if you know it too.

You have been apportioned grace or ability for the fulfilment of your divine assignment. Trying to engage in more than the grace or ability can carry could amount to frustration, futility, and failure. So, be cautious and wise about this. Apostle Paul realized that all things were lawful but not all were beneficial for him. He then chose to do what the grace of God empowered him to do – the needful.

You can only know what things you can do when you put your ability to the test. Put it to work. Yes, it is activity that reveals your true ability. Nobody will truly know your capability until you try your hands on doing something. Make an effort or take up a challenge; that is the way to start.

Unfortunately, some people are afraid of attempting to do something. They defeat themselves by their poor or wrong self-assessment based on past failures at trying to do some things. You should not be. So, do not be afraid to have the encounter otherwise your ability remains uncertain and unrated. After all, no one knows the exact outcome of an encounter until they experience it. Your abilities remain trapped and classless until your potentials are tapped.

One of the things that will help stir you up to try doing something is having knowledge of that thing. To have adequate knowledge or know-how is a leverage. It is a potential that when tapped into proves your ability to succeed at something. But it remains a potential until you put it to use.

For instance, no one will call you an experienced driver until they see you drive on the highways or very busy lanes in the city. This is because the proof of your know-how is in your doing! The proof of your ability is in your activity and accomplishment. You cannot hide and expect the world to believe in what you can do. Those who know do show. Only then can people assess and rate them.

Need for Ability Assessment

It is important to assess your ability to

- ❖ Know what you can really and truly do
- ❖ Know what you really worth
- ❖ Fine-tune your strengths and correct your weaknesses
- ❖ Improve on the measure of grace and faith God has given you
- ❖ Know discover any misconceptions and to correct them.

It is important you do this because God does not use people beyond their know-how and ability. **"Study to show thyself approved unto God"** can better be understood by the next line: **"A workman that needeth not be ashamed but rightly dividing the word of truth"** (2 Timothy 2:15). This is not talking about reading only but working, training, being studious and industrious! Yet these are tied to knowledge. So, to assess your ability, you must use your knowledge profitably and extensively well.

To profit with knowledge, you must believe in yourself. Keep a positive self-image – it is very important. That is, re-assure yourself that you have got something you know that you must show. Publicity attracts patronage! So keep showcasing your knowledge. Keep trying your hands on what you believe you can do and attract positive response. The more you do something, the better you become at it. Then, the higher people get to rate you because they get more convinced of your strong ability.

CHAPTER FIVE

PLANNING

Plan your life and grow rich. Planning is the act of strong reasoning with your pen on paper. You will have no courage or commitment without proper, I mean, serious and adequate planning. Psychology experts have established that planning takes considerable time. It also requires deep thinking with strong willpower. No one plans for the past. Planning is an aspect of preparation for the present and the future. It entails brooding over options, recalling ideas, selecting preferences and working out strategies.

One who must come out with good result must devote time to think. A Toyota advert years ago says, **"Good thinking. Good product."** It is a process of planning. Truth is, it takes all of a man and makes all out of a man. It is real work. Some people will resort to anything to avoid sitting down to think and plan. Others hire people to plan for them because of the labor involved in the process.

Stages of Preparation

There are three stages of every man's life:

- Warming up stage. This is preparation phase; getting your acts ready to launch out
- Winning stage. This is popularity stage; where you are gaining the ground when you have launched out
- Waning stage. At this phase, you are getting set to retire from the stage of activity

But you cannot become popular without solid preparation. This preparation must be by careful and strategic planning, which may take the greater part of your life. And you know, it is worth it. The greater your future, the greater your assignment therefore the greater should your preparation be. I have heard this severally that when preparation meets opportunity, success is inevitable! And it is true.

Poor or inadequate preparation will lead to abuse of opportunity when it finally comes. Remember the popular saying: If you fail to plan, you plan to fail. All-round preparation is essential to winning in your popularity phase of life. Anyone who is not adequately prepared will eventually fail to recognize opportunities. And even when he sees them, he will not be able to grab them because he is not adequately prepared for them.

Planning your future should be based on God's master plan for your life. As a child of God, your future is signposted. And as this statement goes: **"The best thing about the future is that it comes one day at a time"** (Abraham Lincoln). That means you can succeed as you plan one day at a time. Success is not achieved by a magic! It might be stressful and hard to plan now but there cannot be any better thing to do now. This is because **"The better work men do is always done under stress and at a great personal cost"**, says William Carlos Williams.

After moving from a church I co-pioneered and co-pastored for about two years and six months in a part of the country, and subsequently relocating from the area, I began to ask God for direction and another opportunity to do the work of ministry. Before even joining that ministry, I had always updated myself along the lines of my proficiencies. I was well prepared to engage the next opportunity.

Few months after settling down in my new location, I got a new place. Within seven months of being there, I was appointed to stand in for my senior who went on an emergency leave for three full months. While standing in for him, I was appointed to a higher office in the organization. All these happened in about ten months of joining the organization. The leadership found me well-prepared to lead and so gave me the chance.

Necessity for Preparation

The world is fast changing and so a lot of protocols are being sidelined. Adequate preparation becomes essential because

- ❖ Most opportunities come without announcement
- ❖ It discourages laziness and procrastination

❖ It generates better impact than ill-preparation. What it means is that if you must make impact, you must be prepared to work it out.

Success could be heaven-made but the details must be worked out here on earth! There is no magic in arriving at success. You must plan. So, I encourage you to plan and work, if possible, like a slave today and you will live like a king tomorrow! That is what will do the magic.

The ability to plan today is the secret to securing the future tomorrow. Jesus spent about 33 years on earth. The execution of his mission took just about 3 years and some months. That means that he got himself prepared for the greater part of his life. Moses the servant of God spent 120 years on earth: 40 years in Egypt growing up and learning about the land and the people; 40 years in the wilderness under Jethro when he ran away from Egypt; and 40 years executing his mission as a leader of the Israeli nation. That means that he spent two-third of his entire life preparing for his task.

Preparation plus opportunity leads to breakthrough. The following are types of preparation:

- ❖ **Spiritual Preparation**: Your relationship with God matters the most, hence you must take this seriously. There will be no horizontal impact with the world around you without a vertical impact from God on you. God Almighty should come first in your life so you can draw spiritual strength from Him for your assignment. Everything created is spiritual including your assignment. Now imagine God in your corner: success becomes a quick reality. Always remember that!

- ❖ **Intellectual Preparation:** President Solomon David of ancient Israel said, *"Intelligence outranks muscle anytime"* (Proverbs 24:5 TM). A combined dose of knowledge, wisdom and understanding guarantees success to a very large extent. And when sourced from your spiritual standing with God, nothing can stop your success.

- ❖ **Psychological Preparation**: Mental correctness and emotional balance are requirements for achieving stable success. You cannot keep your score high if you cannot keep your mind right. You must learn to prepare and program your mind for success. You achieve this by thinking on what is right, pure, lovely, virtuous and praise-worthy. Keep junks from infesting your mind.

- ❖ **Social Preparation**: Your response to the environment and people is key to attracting success. You are not alone in this world and cannot be oblivious to relationships begging for your attention. What I mean is that you need people and must learn to flow with them in the society. Social life is part of our responsibility to maintain a balanced lifestyle. Create and enjoy circles of friends and families. But as you prepare to engage, you must know when to disengage for your own benefit.

See the future now! Prepare for the long run despite the challenges in the short run. Because the future is always brighter and better than where you are now!

CHAPTER SIX

TRAINING

"I sought employment and found it not because I was without training nor trade that would enable me earn" – The Richest Man in Babylon

I believe that the largest room in the world is the room for self-empowerment. The people we regard and pay homage as masters in their crafts are actually the people who give themselves to knowing more that the average person knows. These people do not rest on their oars until they accomplish their task and even more. What is their little secret? They go for empowerment at every stage of their lives. They do not worry about being criticized about their enthusiasm and the steadfast pursuit of their dreams. And that is why others usually bow before them.

Let me state here that one of the keys to success in your calling and career is getting sound training. You must seek to acquire knowledge through continuous education. Education could be formal or informal. We go to school to get knowledge of some subjects of life such as Mathematics, Biology, etc. However, the practical application of these subjects are not necessarily taught in school; we learn them in informal ways at home, office, etc.

The informal kind of education applies to every stage of life until we are no more. And this is more important than the formal kind. Edward Gibbons confirmed it here: **"Each man receives two types of education; one is given to him courtesy of others, the other and much more important, he gives to himself"**.

Schooling is an aspect of education. However, many are schooled but not *'educated'* while some are educated but not *'schooled'*. Examples of the people who succeeded in life without necessarily passing through the formal education system abound. Even Abraham Lincoln was said to have passed the bar studying at home. What is responsible for this kind of success is when people engage their mental power. The opposite leads to failure or poor result. Mental or intellectual laziness is the reason most people suffer underachievement in their profession or career. So you must study to rise in life.

People who go for training are able to foresee the future. They do not allow the present convenience rob them of the comfort of the future. Oftentimes, people relax after getting to a certain level of success because they feel they have acquired sufficient training to get them settled for the rest of their lives. But sooner or later, they find out that that level of training quickly becomes obsolete and they are out of the system. Therefore, the ability to see beyond the present state is a driving motivation for seeking further knowledge.

Skill Acquisition

You need training in skills. This is also a part of education that everyone should fully embrace. Some are trapped in the middle of a career that has no relationship with the skills they have while many are not employable because they lack needed skills. Anyone who lacks the required skills to pursue a successful career will doubtless end in poverty or in a low life.

I see young people without upgraded and sharpened skills who go into businesses which they will get stuck in due to emerging global trends and competitiveness. This is because they lack concrete skills that would keep them in the system for long. Besides, they may not withstand the competition in the long run. This is why upgraded training is a desirable and non-negotiable option.

Another dimension to training is in the information and communication technology (ICT) sector. In today's emerging world of professional business innovation, there is need for everyone to get quality training in computer and information technology. Unfortunately, so many young and old people that desire success have kept themselves in the dark with respect to this. The only consolation they have is their ability to browse on social media platforms such as Facebook, Instagram, etc. But that is not enough. ICT and the internet world is larger than social media. The social media is just a fraction of the world of internet and ICT. This is very critical especially in this age and time.

Today, virtually all transactions are done through the computer, and in the years to come, it will be very difficult, if not impossible, for anyone without adequate knowledge of the computer to find their feet in either or both the corporate and the business entities.

The opportunities to acquire this specialized training abound all over the world. With a smart phone in hand or a laptop, accessing these opportunities has become so easy to help you improve your standard of living. At least, it will prepare you to have an improved lifestyle in the future. This training will also give you the additional competency to earn the life of your dream.

Proficiency is vital to succeeding in any calling or career. You get this by being consistent and improvising on your area of call. This can happen as you go along – on the job training. You must remember what the richest man in Babylon said, *"I sought employment and found it not because I was without training nor trade that would enable*

me earn." You must not let this statement be your experience. It is indeed a sad story!

Revisit Your Course

One of the ways to keep yourself in training mode is by revisiting your course. Some people throw away their course materials once they graduate from high school or the university. All that occupies their mind is to make money without realizing that it is increased knowledge of their profession that brings in the cash flow. I discovered that repetition is the precursor of retention, and retention produces perfection. So, one more time, I advise that you revisit your course!

Training and re-training yourself in the line of your career usually comes with a cost which might be discouraging at first. However, the number of years you decide to invest in training despite a discouraging present is one of the greatest factors in actualizing your future dream.

Training is progressive, not a one-time thing. So you should be ready to respond spontaneously. However, training yourself should not be a do-or-die affair but a live-and-do affair! All you need is the right attitude – and that is, learning how to unlearn some things and to learn new things. This is because the things which at the beginning made you successful might not necessarily keep you on that level of success. Formulas are usually revisited from time to time. So, do not depend on yesterday's success formula for it might not guarantee today's breakthrough.

It is possible to train yourself. This is my advice: If you are not privileged to have anybody train you in formal education, get a skill. Look for a mentor to teach you what you need to know to stay relevant. And if no one is there to train you, then you should train yourself. If you cannot get it by the school, then, get it by the books! Go to the internet and you will see a whole lot of free materials on various courses and people who are waiting to engage you.

Training from Experience

Apart from the conventional training, you can also receive training through what you experience. Life can take you through some processes that would leave you better if you choose to respond with right attitude. For instance, facing challenges develops your virtues and sharpen your skills to help you in future pursuits. You gain experience through this kind of training and you also become stronger when you overcome overwhelming situations.

It is rightly said that the school of experience will repeat the lesson if you fail the first time. The intention of that training is not to fail you but to test your abilities and make you more resourceful. But if you fail to pass it, you will have a *"carry-over"* that might become a heavy burden to bear. Face it when you have the strength otherwise you may not escape it when it comes to the crunch.

Prophet Jeremiah said, **"It is a good thing for a man to bear his burden in his youth**"- Lamentations 3:27. It is not an easy ride to say the least but grace for the training is available to you.

The paradox is that when we allow anything to succeed in shielding us from immediate pain, that thing also prevents us from learning how to reduce the causes of the pain. Yes, that is right! Running away from a painful experience is a lack of understanding of the fact that it is through that experience that we know its cause and solution. The book of Hebrews chapter five and verse eight said that through suffering, Jesus learned obedience. Malcolm X once told his attorney a story which he summarized in the words: **"You may run and hide; you may turn and twist, but you cannot get out of this life alive!"** So then, you have to face it!

If you know that tough times do not last, then you will allow what you encounter to teach you how to cope with tough times when they come. Surely, they must come. To be able to go through them, you must develop steel courage.

Another factor you may also need to employ is a bit of compromise. Compromise on your personal philosophy may not be a bad idea in order to go through certain experiences. You may not always hold tight onto your principles especially when they are not working out good success. There should be room for adjustment. You cannot always remain like rigid; employ a bit of flexibility so you can achieve more of your dreams. This makes you wise, not foolish.

Never mind those who may come up to bother you by calling you a compromiser. They have their own opinions. According to Ralph Waldo Emerson, **"Whatever course you decide upon, there's always someone to tell you you're wrong. There are always difficulties arising which tempt you to believe that your critics are right."** Just be sure that you are not compromising in areas that need you to stand on your convictions. But rather in areas that could pitch you against sound, standard practices. And do not allow their tantrums or bigoted opinions rob you of opportunities to achieve your dream success.

Courage in Training

Most of the training that will get you above average might be very hard and crushingly demanding. In this case, you need a lot of courage. This is because you get better when you respond with courage to challenges than when we face them with fear. You stand to benefit in the following ways:

- ❖ Courage will help you to face the truth about yourself. You do not need to be scared of facing some sad or painful realities about yourself. Shying away from addressing those negatives can jeopardize future efforts to make progress.

- ❖ It will help you to move from your comfort zone to take a step of faith. You should not be satisfied with the level of success you have reached. Even the world's richest men still want to make more money. The higher you go, the safer you become, and the more impact you are likely to make in life. So courageously quit your comfort zone.

- ❖ It will help you to stand for your convictions when they are being challenged*. Taking a stand for what you believe is never a joke especially when dealing with aggressive opposition. But if you must succeed, you need to employ courage and faith to stand out, and not to blend in.

Ask God for the courage to go through whatever situation that seems challenging and tough. He is your God and will always stand with you no matter what if you trust Him.

The Holy Bible states, **"So we're not giving up. How could we! ...it often looks like things are falling apart on us, on the inside,...God is making new life, ...These hard times are small potatoes compared to the coming good times, the lavish celebration prepared for us"** – 2 Corinthians 4:16-17 TM. If you must become a celebrity, then you cannot escape the training! It is worth the sacrifice.

CHAPTER SEVEN

DISCOVERY

"Eureka!" That was what someone exclaimed when he found something. ***"Behold! I do a new thing..."*** says the Lord because He discovered a new way.

Some people tend to continue to do the same things over and again even when they are not making any positive headway. When you try and fail, try again and fail, you need to pause and ask some vital questions. It could be that you need to change the path or pattern, be more pragmatic, and approach the matter from another angle. This usually takes honesty, openness, and calculated effort and you have to be ready to do it. Do you know why?

Change Needs Fresh Ideas

Some people want to succeed but are not ready to change. Even when they are ready to change, they do not wish to change completely. They still feel some things should remain the way they are. If the change you make does not bring the success you desire, change again. You cannot put new wine in old wineskin because the old wineskin does not have the strength to hold the fervor of the new wine.

Discovering new things is the secret of changing the world. New ideas must be presented in fresh new packages for people to embrace and appreciate them. Grace cannot wed the Law, neither can it flourish on the grounds of legalism. In the same way, not only should you discover new things, but you must make them appealing to those who you wish to embrace them. Some who say you do not judge a book by its cover may be right in some sense. However, truth remains that people hardly buy what is not attractive to their eyes.

Factors Leading to Discovery

Now, there are some factors that can lead you to any kind of discovery. One of them is **dissatisfaction.** When you are dissatisfied with where you are, your business, level of career success or state of your environment, this has the tendency to drive your into research and study on how to change the narratives. Dissatisfaction breeds unhappiness. And this state of unhappiness brings with it restlessness and the urge to do something positive. So when you now launch out for solutions, you are bound to discover them. This break often brings you joy and others come to celebrate your feat.

Another factor that leads to discovery is quest for knowledge. Most of the discoveries by some scientists came as results of quest to know more that they know. This kind of discovery can be termed adventurous discovery. The experience and discoveries of President Solomon David as recorded in his Quester (Ecclesiastes) are good examples of this kind of discovery. The wisest man that lived on earth found more than he intended to know, and that is why today, we have his works and words chronicled in the most widely read book in the universe.

There is still one other thing that can drive someone into discovery. It is fear of death. Yes, you heard me right. The fear of dying early led to the discoveries of longevity pills. The fear of ageing quick has also led to the discovery and making of anti-ageing formulas that keep people looking younger than their real age.

But there is still another angle to this fear. Perhaps, this is the most enthusing of them all.

You know about Jacob the son of Isaac the son of Abraham the friend of God in the Bible. When he was running away from Esau who threatened to kill him, he came to a place where he spent the night. Unknowing to him, the place was a holy place. He did not know that he was right at a place of encounter with his Creator. When he found out he exclaimed, **"This is none other than the house of God, and I did not know it!"**- Gen. 28:13 NKJV. Thank God it was not when he had left the place that Bethel was discovered.

Jacob discovered Bethel. He changed its name from Luz to Bethel. Someone else would have done that if he was not on the lookout. Imagine how awful you would feel if you found out that what you could have discovered was discovered by someone else. And it does not get better if it is someone you are better than in many ways. The feeling is usually painful. That is why you are to always get your eyes peeled for such chances that can register your name on the right side of history. This is super success, if you ask me.

The place called Dubai today was just a barren land in the heart of Arabian Desert several years ago. But someone saw a future attraction center. Today, Dubai has become a reference point in global development. You do not have to look too far for you to discover something that has the potential of turning your dream into reality and launching you to the center stage of relevance. Such opportunities abound everywhere you turn. Just open your eyes!

Discover People for Profit

The highest form of investment that guarantees high premiums is people investment or investment in people. We should not only discover things or places, but also people with quality ideas. You may be a businessman who is interested in manufacturing, buying and selling products but if you could look around you, there are people with ideas you could turn into products and services. If you are an investor, there may be people around you who are potential investment opportunities walking the streets. All you need do is to discover them and invest in their ideas. There are people who could turn you into a millionaire if you could discover and invest in them.

Are you looking for new ways to increase your earnings and improve your life? Then, discover someone. I know this involves a lot of risks, but you must be ready to make the needed move. If you do not make timely advances, you will miss the golden chances. The painful part is if your competitor dares what scares you and succeeds. It really pains – a lot.

The reason God planted those people around you is for you to discover them; what you can gain from them by giving what they need to gain from you. There is no coincidence or accident with this kind of divine arrangement. God has concluded all about you. You just have to find it out by yourself. Success does not just come to us, we should go for it!

So, what do you do? You should not just look but try hard to see. You should not just think, try to ponder. Do more than acknowledge, identify with them. Do not talk about how you would have done it but how you did. If you cannot win at the moment, please help someone to win and so become a part of the winning team! Joseph did that in prison; he interpreted dreams with pleasure and his free service later brought him a life of leisure. Only those who think other than themselves can see opportunity to discover other people.

One thing I do all my life is to be on the lookout for opportunities to become a part of people's success. I tell you, many a people that I have come across cannot talk about their successes without mentioning my name whether in the ministry or in other aspects of life. Remember, success is not measured by the amount of money you have got in your bank account but the number of people you support to succeed in their calling and career. The degree of joy and depth of fulfilment in carrying out the will of God is what counts.

Discover Yourself for Posterity

Discovery for success could come in another form. Yes, there is discovery of people and things. There is also discovery of self. Self-discovery is an outcome of an experience-riddled life. Your true self usually manifests when you are put through a process; usually under pressure. Most people do not know their true worth until they go through some challenging experiences. Most talented and gifted people that are successful discovered their unique selling points during trying moments. I am one of them. You may know some other people, too.

Success is the fulfilment of a desire, an aspiration, a dream or a vision. Success is not the acquisition of material things. It is not the amassing of wealth but the completion of a God-given assignment or a personal ambition according to the will of God.

A successful person is one who, in the process of fulfilling his potentials, receives recognition, earns good money, and makes a difference in the lives of other people. You will always be remembered for one of these: those you put on stage, those you brought down from stage, or those you ignored and did nothing to help up stage. *"Had I known"* is a product of negligence because with or without you, those destined to be on stage will surely be there. Would it not rather be a privilege to be credited for putting someone on stage?

Success does not come to the man who idly waits for it but the man who earnestly goes for it by discovering ways to succeed. Discover today what to do to add meaning to the society and your own life will be full of meaning. Here is my advice: Take the pains to do so now and get ready to enjoy the gains later. I bet you think so.

CHAPTER EIGHT

VISION

"If I have seen farther than others, it is because I have stood on the shoulders of giants." – Newton

The power of imagination and expression; wisdom in understanding the true meaning of facts, especially with regard to the future, a beautiful picture seen in the mind; idea, especially as a fulfilment of a desire, that is what vision is all about.

To have a vision means to have something worth living for or dying for. Apostle Paul said, **"To live is Christ, and to die is gain"**. This was because he had a vision. Every man will end up becoming what he can see of himself. If you visualize a great one of yourself, you will doubtless become a great one. Setbacks or no setbacks, if you stick to your vision, only time will prove you victorious. After all, setbacks provide us with the opportunity to pause, plan and push again.

The Concept of Vision

To have the power of imagination is essential in becoming successful in life. No one is a success until he achieves his God-given vision. There are things you see which no other person sees. You imagine things that only you understand. When you talk about these things, some folks laugh at you. But, hey, they are there in your mind all the time. They are not just imagination, but vision.

You can also call them impressions. Apart from seeing them in your imagination, you feel they are impressed in your heart. You think about them, and sometimes wonder how to get them out. That is where expression comes in. This is where the struggle also comes in. I will discuss that later.

So you must visualize it all, and arrange them in the way they come to you. You can write all those impressions down and begin to study them. Charles M. Schwab said, **"For a man to carry out a successful business, he must have imagination. He must be able to see things in a vision; must have a dream of the whole thing."** To have the dream of the whole thing enhances your ability to focus. This is the power of foresight. It means that you cannot rule the future you do not see in the present.

There are two kinds of vision though. One is given by God while the other you create for yourself. The former is usually bigger than you and can only be actualized by supernatural ability. The one you design by yourself is often something you take on according to your abilities. Whichever, vision will take all of you with God's help to achieve.

Vision and What It Takes

Having a clear-cut vision, however, is not all a man needs to succeed. Vision needs provision. It must be matched by action. This is because vision without action becomes a daydream. That is to say, you must give expression to your impression – those imaginations swimming in your subconscious mind.

Your vision may require a non-conventional means to actualize it. It may be a crazy idea or approach but it is not altogether evil. I find that following certain protocols many a times has proved elusive and in some cases, counterproductive. That is the point. I do not subscribe to breaking the rules in order for you to achieve your goal but note that rules are made to guide and not to god us!

In the Bible book of Judges 14:1-4, God was thinking of how to assail the Philistines who at the time subjugated the Israelites. One way He found to do it was such that did not go well with common sense.

"Samson went down to Timnah and at Timnah saw one of the daughters of the Philistines. And he came up and told his father and mother, I saw one of the daughters of the Philistines at Timnah; now get her for me as my wife. But his father and mother said to him, Is there not a woman among the daughters of your kinsmen or among all our people, that you must go to take a wife from the uncircumcised Philistines? And Samson said to his father, Get her for me, for she is all right in my eyes. His father and mother did not know that it was of the Lord, and that He sought an occasion for assailing the Philistines. At that time the Philistines had dominion over Israel." (Amplified Bible)

It sounds crazy that God would think of using this means to deal with the enemies of His people. But that is God for you. So even if it is a "crazy" idea, remember, it is not evil at all. However, it is only God that can give you the best way of accomplishing your vision. God's idea of the 'how' may not appeal or answer to everybody's 'why'. So, do not be swayed by people's opinion or reaction. Just follow the idea as it comes as long as it does not hurt anyone. You do not need to step on heads to get to the top. Use the ladder instead.

Vision and Deadlines

A vision is not developed in a day. It takes time to conceive, nurture, and achieve it. The time varies with the magnitude of the vision. Every woman's pregnancy has a period of nine months before delivery. This is a constant. Nevertheless, not all that conceive the same day give birth on the same day.

There are seasons for all visions. Your vision has a season to be actualized. Ignorance of this truth has made many people to think that spiritual exercise such as fasting or prayer performs magic. Truth is: Fasting and prayer will not force the vision to happen before its time, but will help you to wait for its time of actualization. God told Habakkuk, **"Write the** *vision…"* but *"if it seems slow in coming, wait. It's on its way. It will come right on time"* – Habakkuk 2:2-3 **(The Message).** So there is a waiting period. You cannot hurry the process.

Your vision must have a deadline; a date set to achieve it. When I was thinking of getting married, I had no dime. In fact, my bank account was reading almost zero dollars. Someone told me to fix a day for the wedding and it would hold. A year before, I chose a date even though I had not yet met my wife. With that date set and my mind set on that date, I planned and prayed for my wedding.

I had told God that I would meet my wife before or on my birthday of that year – and I met my wife four days to my birthday. My wife was actually a birthday present from God and I wedded her six months later. it was exactly the day I had earlier set for it. That is the power of setting a deadline, and exercising faith for the actualization of your vision. Your success may delay if you do not set time for your dream.

Stretch it Further

If you must do the incredible stuffs in life, you must think the impossible and dream of breaking your own records. To do this, you must demand the impossible from your brain. Your brain has been wired to think out solutions beyond what you could possibly imagine. So when you have a vision and set out to achieve it, it behooves on you to place strong realistic demands on your brain to give you expected results. Only those who ask for the impossible often get the best result. After all, it is never an offence to stretch ones imagination. It is a gift of God.

"After Lot was gone, the LORD said to Abram, "Look as far as you can see in every direction" – Gen. 13:14 TLB. God encourages extra mile. You can do more than you have been doing. You do not need to be a Jack of all trades but being a Jack of many trades is not a bad idea. Do not let anyone talk you into a mediocre life. What you need is focus, then add determination to it, and you can achieve anything. Visualize it all at a time, and then actualize it one at a time.

When You Lack Vision

"Where there is no vision, the people perish..."
"For lack of wood the fire goes out..." (Proverbs 29:18; 26:20 AMP).

Most people wonder why their lives lack great accomplishment. The answer is in those two wise sayings of President Solomon David of ancient Israel. You may be a potential millionaire but if you are not seeing the big picture, you might end a pauper, the secret to great success lies in your sight. What you see is what you seek, and what you seek is what you receive. There is no going around it. It is an unchangeable principle of life on earth.

There was darkness all over the pre-creation world, but God saw light. And when he spoke what He saw, light appeared out of darkness. If you keep seeing a miserable future, you end up attracting misery and living a miserable life. Vision controls passion and passion directs action. So when you lack quality vision, you lack strong passion and what you get is lame action. You know what, this will get you nowhere near success.

Efficacy of Vision

Having said much about vision, let me say this in conclusion: Vision will give you stability in life. Vision will adjust your behavior and character. It will give focus that is definite and direct. It gives motivation for your pursuit. Vision gives desire. It is desire that leads to enquiry. And when you enquire you can surely acquire your desire.

Vision is so powerful that it creates room for strategy. To strategize means to visualize the most effective means of achieving your goal or dream. This, however, requires that you exercise your mind and imaginative ability in a definite direction towards the goal. So, expand your horizon and see beyond your scope.

CHAPTER NINE

TIME AND CHANCE

"I returned and saw under the sun that the race is not to the swift nor the battle to the strong, neither is bread to the wise nor riches to men of intelligence and understanding nor favor to men of skill; but time and chance happen to them all"
– Ecclesiastes 9:11 Amplified Bible

The Psalmist David Jesse noted in Psalm 33:16 that no king is saved by the great size and power of his army. He further observed that a mighty man is not delivered by his much strength. What this means in this context is that success is not by might or power, but by time and chance. Yes, God decides outcomes but you can decide otherwise if you miss your time and chance. This is what I will discuss with you in this chapter. You must not miss out any point here.

The Concept of Time and Chance

According to Plato and Aristotle, time is a measurable succession governed principally by the movement of the heavenly bodies. This is objective experience. Bergson thought of time as concrete duration, the experience of time from within. This is subjective experience. Time therefore is both objective and subjective.

The Greek rendering of time gives the clue of two types of time. *"Chronos"* (Greek: χρόνος) meaning *"clock time"* is formally sequential or chronological time while *"Kairos"* means right time. In Ancient Greek, Kairos "καιρός" means 'the right, critical, or opportune moment'. In Modern Greek, Kairos also means 'weather'.

Time gives direction. It produces seasons. See Ecclesiastes 3:1, **"To everything there is a season, and a time for every matter or purpose under heaven"** (AMP). Time is the rate at which direction flows or travels through a season. Everyone has got a season for performance. Understanding the time of your season is the key to great performance in life. Like the tribe of Issachar who had the understanding of the times to give command to their brethren on what to do and when to do what, you stand to be a leader in your generation.

People heal at different rates. They also move at different speeds. There is no competition in destiny. You just have to understand the purpose of God for your life, the season He has designed for its fulfilment, and the duration of the season. All seasons do not have equaled timing so also the life of man.

Chance is the occurrence of an event. It is also an atmosphere for the performance of an event. The meeting point of time and chance is what I can describe as opportunity. Opportunity is the chance to perform an event within a given time. A chance for advancement. A circumstance suitable for a particular purpose. It is a gift from God to show forth one's favorite qualities, potentials, talents, and gifts.

Recognizing Opportunities

Everyone you know that has succeeded in life got the opportunity. It is either you are given opportunity or that you seek out opportunity. But the fact remains that it comes to everyone at a particular time of life.

The unfortunate thing is that you may have missed many a great opportunity for you to record mind-blowing success. I have missed some, too. And it is no fun to miss hitting the jackpot, trust me.

When someone around you complains of facing a challenge, it is an opportunity to proffer a way out. When someone tells you that he is suffering from an ailment, opportunity is being given to you to introduce a cure. Esau was hungry and asked for food; Jacob saw an opportunity of getting the birth right. This is part of my coaching classes I call, Business Intelligence.

Joseph saw the opportunity of introducing his talent in prison. He interpreted the dreams of Pharaoh's chief butler and chief baker at no charge! Two years later, he was invited by one of them to the king's palace, and he was made the prime minister.

When the pastor calls for building support, it is an opportunity to lend to God. When you see a talented person full of ideas who does not have the money to sponsor it, you are being offered an opportunity to negotiate a deal that would favor and benefit both of you.

When you see a frustrated fellow, you have the opportunity to minister help like Jesus did. **"I was hungry …you gave me food. I was thirsty …you gave me drink. I needed clothes…you gave me. I was sick and you visited me."** Matt. 25:35-36). The people that respond to the need of others respond to opportunity they see.

Everyone, at one time or the other, has been offered opportunity to do something. Your problem, I suppose, may be that you did not recognize them as great opportunities. Do not be like the Jews and their Pharisee leaders who kept expecting the messiah even when He was right in their midst. The power of recognition is not in your eyes but in your mind! You see with your eyes but recognize with your mind.

People who achieve success in life do so by grabbing the opportunities that come their way. Most of us pray that God should make us rich and wealthy but the answer is that we should open our eyes to opportunities. You pray for the spirit of patience, try to maintain your place in a queue and sometimes allow others to go first. You can also learn to wait on God and others until they are ready to give you attention. Do not always be in a hurry! **"Haste makes waste!"** (Proverbs)

Recognizing opportunity is the starting point of achieving great things. There are people in around the world that saw the opportunity to invest in potential projects and people and they seized the moment.

Jesus Christ saw the future of His ministry in the hands of fishermen like Peter, Andrew, James and John, and He invested His time and anointing in them. Today, we cannot divorce those apostles from the ministry or name of Jesus. Be like-minded!

The Challenge with Opportunity

Most people want to really seize the moment and make meaningful success. But they have a challenge with knowing which one is the chance they should take. You may even say, 'Well, a chance like that has not been given me'. But that is not true. According to my finding, most opportunities come without announcement. At other times, they come in sack-cloth in the form of work or service. You have had your chances but you despised and discarded them as insignificant. And you did forget that most insignificant things have led to glorious and magnificent victories. Check the history books.

It was the idea of a Hebrew slave girl that gave Naaman his healing. See Old Testament book of 2 Kings 5:3, **"Now the bands of raiders from Aram had gone out and had taken captive a young girl from Israel, and she served Naaman's wife. She said to her mistress, "If only my master would see the prophet who is in Samaria! He would cure him of his leprosy."** Naaman almost missed the chance of getting healed of his leprosy if not for the persuasion of his servants (5:13). He was considering his prestigious position in the society but failed to consider his ugly condition as a leper. That was a poor mentality and mind-set!

You may have the money; yes, you are rich but may not be known until you seize the opportunity to raise someone who can make you known. The world is not looking for rich men but men who are known for making others rich and known. I learnt something from a story about Bill Gate, the American rich man at the time. The story was told that an unnamed reporter interviewed Bill Gates and asked the billionaire, "What is the secret of your success?"

Instead of giving an answer, Bill Gates signed a blank check from his personal checkbook and handed it to the reporter telling him to write whatever amount he wanted on it. But the reporter rejected the check and went on with the question. So Gates told him that the secret of his success was to never miss an opportunity.

Imagine if that reporter had recognized that moment as his "Kairos", he would probably had become one of the richest journalists in the world.

All that happens in life is by time and chance. Reading this book and learning the wisdom in it to succeed is an opportunity given which you have seized already.

If you did not take the chance, you might not know all these things. Just know that now is the time and you have a chance. Seize it and succeed!

CHAPTER TEN

MAKE THE RIGHT CHOICE

"See, I set before you today life and prosperity, death and destruction." Deuteronomy 30:15 NIV

Choice is an aspect of moral goodness – an act of **"true virtue which is not possible for an automation or for a non-human organism, but for a being with reason, will, freedom, and moral responsibility"** – Aristotle (emphasis mine).

Choice is the condition of moral virtue. The Greek term *"proairesis"*, which means the choosing of one thing before or in preference to another thing, signals a process of previous deliberation. Aristotle added that **"Choice, then, is a deliberate desire of things in our own power, for when we have decided as a result of deliberation, we desire in accordance with our deliberation."**

Choice and Responsibility

Choice is not a mere wish or an opinion. It is a deliberate choosing or selection of things. Some people intentionally choose rightly out of good character while others deliberately choose wrongly due to bad lifestyle. We all make our choices of where to live, what to do, and how to do what we want to. You are free to choose how to manage your resources as long as it does not violate divine principles for living. If you are a Christian, your interests should align with God's will and purpose.

Everyone has their interests. It is not a bad thing to express what you really want. We will only produce frustration when we pretend not to seek our own interests in doing some things or carrying out some actions. What is important is that you consult widely before making your final decision on any subject or matter of interest.

According to Adam Smith, *"**Every man is free to pursue his own interest his own way as long as he does not violate the laws of justice.**"* Our greatest resource lies in what we enjoy doing as long as it does not harm other people.

Commenting in his book *'Free to Choose'*, Milton Friedman says, **"No one should be prevented from (pursuing and) achieving those positions for which their talents (abilities, potentials, proficiencies) fit them and which their values lead them."**

Although you have the freedom to choose yet you must consider your responsibility to other people. This responsibility is the ability to deny yourself some things which you have the right to choose or respond to but which may negatively affect others.

Any choice that does not promote love, unity, peace, and progress of your family and the society is not a worthy option. You should care about the choices you make. You must remember that when you choose a course, you equally choose the consequences or benefits attached to that course.

So the choices and decisions you make are responsible for the end you get. The Almighty God has set before us options and given us the freedom to choose. (Deuteronomy 30:15-20) He wants His plans for you to run unhindered but the wrong choices you make might disrupt the execution of those plans. Thus, it affects you as well as others whose destinies are tied to yours. After all, the essence of living is not for self but in living for others. In my opinion, anyone who does otherwise is not really wise! Philanthropists get more and more because they live more for others than for self.

Jesus says, **"If anyone desires to come after me, let him deny himself, and take up his cross daily and follow me"** – Luke 9:23 NKJV. **"For even the Son of Man did not come to be served, but to serve, and to give His life a ransom for many"** – Mark 10:45 NKJV. The key phrase there is "to serve and to give His life a ransom for many". This is the right model for living.

"…Choose you this day whom ye will serve…" is an invitation to make a choice, **"but as for me and my house, we will serve the Lord"** is an example of the right choice made. The last line is this: Make the right choices and success will knock on your door!

CONCLUSION

Success is everyone's dream. To succeed in life's calling and career is the will of God for all people. No one wants to identify with failures even if they are their family members. But to succeed requires intelligence. To me, intelligence is captured in the following scripture: **"It takes wisdom to build a house, and understanding to set it on a firm foundation; it takes knowledge to furnish its rooms with fine furniture and beautiful draperies. It's better to be wise than strong: intelligence outranks muscle any day. Strategic planning is the key to warfare; to win, you need a lot of good counsel."**

Check out these quotes from the chapters of this book. One or two will definitely charge you towards succeeding in life.

"The ability to plan today is the key to securing the future tomorrow."

"Training yourself should not be a do-or-die affair but a live-to-do affair."

"If you cannot get it by the school, get it by the books!"

"If you do not take the risk, do not expect the yield."

"God can only give attention to the man who is focused."

"The proof of your know-how is in your do-now!"

"The best way to be the best is to remain the best you are made to be!"

"If you cannot win at the moment, help someone to win and so become part of the winning team."

"God's idea of *the how* may not appeal to everybody's *why*."

"A crazy idea, sometimes, is not evil."

"Don't be a Jack of all trades, but being a Jack of many trades is not an offence."

THE LAST LINE

I believe that this book has tremendously touched and ministered to you. God is pointing us to a life of fulfilment and if you are not there yet, do not throw in the towel because there is still hope for you. God has called us to a life of accomplishment through the grace that He has given. So, it is our responsibility to live that life to the fullest.

That life cannot be lived in the flesh but in the spirit. That is Christianity. So, if you are yet to become a believer in Jesus Christ, do not wait for long. The time (Kairos) is NOW for you to become born again. No life can match the life of godliness. Believe me, there is no real life outside Christ!

So as you strive to succeed by the wisdom you have learned from reading this book, make sure that you do so by the help of God through Jesus Christ. Remember, he that does otherwise is not wise!

You can send your feedback to this email: palacemedia338@hgmail.com; buy and read other resources by this same author on www.amazon.com/author/palacemedia_22books

REFERENCES

All scripture quotations are from the Holy Bible: Authorized Kings James Version (KJV) Red Letter Edition.

Verses marked TLB are taken from The Living Bible, copyright@1971. Used by permission of Tyndale House Publishers, Inc. Wheaton, Illinois 60189. All rights reserved.

Verses marked (TM) are taken from The Message, copyright@ 1993, 1994, 1995, 1996, 2000, 2001, 2002.

Verses marked (AMP) are from the Amplified Bible

Verses marked (NIV) are from the New International Version

The Word for Today by Bob Gass, September 2008

Wikipedia online dictionary

www.ingramcontent.com/pod-product-compliance
Lightning Source LLC
Chambersburg PA
CBHW070254220526
45465CB00004B/1622